# Holidays at a Country Home

by Judy Condon

©2011 Marsh Homestead Country Antiques

Library of Congress Cataloging-in-Publications Data
Holidays at a Country Home by Judy Condon
ISBN 978-0-9843332-7-1

Oceanic Graphic Printing, Inc.
105 Main Street
Hackensack, NJ 07601

Printed in China

Layout and Design by Pat Lucas
Edited by Trent Michaels

# Table of Contents

# About the Author

Judy Condon is a native New Englander, which is evident in her decorating style and the type of antiques she collects and sells. Her real passion is 19thC authentic dry red or blue painted pieces. While Judy enjoyed a professional career as a teacher, Principal and Superintendent of Schools in Connecticut, Judy's weekends were spent at her antique shop, *Marsh Homestead Country Antiques*, located in Litchfield, Connecticut.

When her husband, Jeff, was relocated to Virginia, Judy accepted an early retirement from education and concentrated her energy and passion for antiques into a fulltime business. Judy maintains a website, *www.marshhomesteadantiques.com* and has been a Power Seller on ebay® for over thirteen years under the name "superct".

Judy and her husband Jeff recently returned to their roots in New England and are in the process of renovating a 19thC home in Massachusetts which will be included in a near future book. Judy has five children and five grandchildren and enjoys reading, golf, Bridge, tennis and volunteering in the educational system in St Maarten. Judy has been in the process of providing teaching materials and children's books to the schools in St. Maarten with the hopes of helping to establish classroom libraries.

Judy's first sixteen books in the "simply country" series, *Country on a Shoestring, Of Hearth and Home–Simply Country, A Simpler Time, Country Decorating for All Seasons, As Time Goes By, Country at Heart, Welcome Home–Simply Country, Home Again–Simply Country, The Warmth of Home, The Country Home, The Comfort of Home, Simple Greens–Simply Country, The Country Life, Simply Country Gardens, The Spirit of Country,* and *The Joy of Country* have been instant hits and most are already in their second printing. Judy may be reached through her website *www.marshhomesteadantiques.com*, her email address, *marshhomestead @comcast.net* or by phone at 877-381-6682.

# *Our Christmas on Wheels*

Is there anywhere we would rather be for the holidays than that place we call home?

Every holiday song speaks of the excitement of Christmas, the bustle, children's eyes wide with wonder, stockings hung by the fire, carolers, holly and mistletoe, and the spirit of good cheer that we all wish would last the entire year.

My family is blessed with longevity. As a result, when my children were very young, we had a number of Christmas celebrations and stops to make; we usually began our holiday trek December 23, which enabled us to celebrate with four sets of grandparents and great-grandparents. My children, now all in their 40's, retain fractions of special memories from each visit. Although they can't always recall which great-grandparent we were visiting at the time, they remember a little room where they enjoyed a small tree with bubbling lights, the kitchen table that featured a glass of milk and a cut-out cookie, or the unique angel tree topper.

While my children laugh at what they now call "Our Christmas on wheels", the best celebration was the one at home with cookies for Santa, carrots for the reindeer, and the exclamations of delight at dawn.

I spoke of my family's traditions in *Country Decorating for All Seasons* but neglected to mention our Christmas morning breakfast tradition – homemade cinnamon rolls, or as we call them, "sticky buns". I first made them over 45 years ago and the honor has now passed to my daughters. We enjoy them only once a year and look forward with watering mouths and great anticipation. On the next page is my recipe, which I'd like to share with you despite the fact that my eldest grandson Matthew was appalled that Grammy would divulge the secret recipe! Try it if you dare!

# Sticky Buns

## Sweet Dough:

| | |
|---|---|
| 1/2 cup milk | 1/2 cup sugar |
| 1/2 teaspoon salt | 1/4 cup butter |
| 1/2 cup warm water | 2 packages cake yeast |
| 2 eggs beaten | 3-1/2 cups sifted flour |

Scald milk. Stir in sugar, salt, margarine and cool to a lukewarm temperature. Measure the warm water into a large warm bowl. Crumble and sprinkle the yeast into the water, stirring until the yeast is totally dissolved. Add the yeast mixture to the milk mixture.

Add the beaten eggs and half the flour to the lukewarm milk mixture. Beat until smooth. Stir in the remaining flour to produce slightly stiff dough. Turn the dough out on a lightly floured board. Knead until smooth and elastic (about eight minutes).

Place dough in a greased bowl, turning to grease both sides. Cover with a towel and let rise in a warm place free from draft until the dough doubles in bulk (approximately one hour).

Punch down and turn out on a floured board.

## Topping:

1 cup butter
2-1/2 cups brown sugar
1/2 cup pecans (optional)
1 teaspoon cinnamon

I add a little maple syrup and vanilla to topping once it melts.

Melt butter and stir in 1-1/2 cups brown sugar, 1/2 teaspoon cinnamon, and optional pecans.

Grease pans and pour half of the melted topping into the bottom of the pan. Set aside.

Mix remaining 1 cup brown sugar, 1/2 teaspoon cinnamon.

Divide dough in half. Roll out each half to a 12" square. Sprinkle each half with the dry brown sugar and cinnamon mix. Drizzle the remaining melted topping on the squares.

Roll up lengthwise as a jelly roll and cut into 1" slices. Place in the prepared pans.

Cover and let rise in a warm place until doubled in bulk (approximately one hour).

Bake in a pre-heated oven at 350 degrees for 25 minutes.

These can be made ahead and frozen, then heated on Christmas morning in a low heat oven.

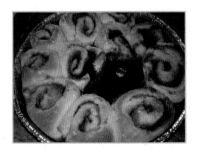

# Chapter 1

❋

# *Kari and Jack Cameron*

Kari and Jack Cameron's home in Waukesha, Wisconsin, was built in 1994 by Kari's son Tim Miller, a preservation carpenter; he is also Leeds certified, which means that he builds entire homes with recycled materials. Kari and Jack built on a former 19thC farmstead. In fact, Kari operates a shop, *Just a Little Bit Country*, in the original summer kitchen of the farmhouse. Another original building houses *Smokehouse Primitives*, an extension of her shop. Kari is available for interior decorating consultation specific to the period. She has been in business for 27 years and also designs hooked rug patterns which she sells through another business called *Log Cabin Rugs* available through her shop website *www.justalittlebitcountry.com*.

Jack also operates a café on the property.

Kari and Jack's home is a perfect example of what can be achieved with greenery strategically placed throughout the house during the holiday season. Kari says she is color sensitive, as she often creates her own colors by mixing samples until she achieves the exact look she needs. The outside of the house is painted a sandy taupe, a special mix of Kari's. The exterior trim is a "Barn Red" by Olde Century.

Kari, like many of us, mixes authentic antiques with reproduction country accessories. The trim paint in the foyer is Sherwin-Williams "Besom Broom" and is used throughout most of the house. The four-drawer chest is New England and all original, and dates to the late 1700's or early 1800's. Kari suspects that, based on the clothing, the portrait was painted after the sitter was deceased – a common practice in the mid to late 18thC.

The redware pitcher is early. Both the candlestand on the right and the Windsor chair are reproductions. The paneling throughout the house and the staircase were hand-hewn by Tim.

The bottom piece is an immigrant trunk dated 1857. The portrait of a young girl is dated 1826. The coverlets on the chair and hanging from the peg rack are both mid-19thC and dated.

Kari purchased the Federal tall case grandfather clock with a period finish from the Ohio River Valley Company.

Pomegranates in a wire basket hang above a pumpkin pine 19thC dry sink in the back hall. The black iron pump is original to the sink.

While the hunt board on the back stair landing is a new piece, everything on and around it is early. The piece in the corner looks like a churn but is actually an early storage piggin.

The mantel in the Gathering Room is filled with a combination of new and old pewter plates. The candlemold at the end is early as is the decoy on the left. The musket is dated 1830.

Every piece on the hearth is an early cooking utensil or container. A sap bucket holds an assortment of greenery, berries, and pods.

Kari surrounds the base of her tree in the corner with an assortment of early toys including this child's dapple glider horse.

Kari burns many candles during the year and saves the nubs to place in the tin candleholders on the holiday tree.

The game table is a Laurence Crouse piece. The reproduction black Windsor chairs were purchased at The Seraph.

Ratchet hand-wrought iron candleholders made by Kathy Nugent of Primitives hang on either side of an early 1800's oil portrait above the sofa.

Kari sells many of the quilt racks, shown above, in her shop. Another beautiful mid-19thC coverlet looks striking against the greenery and lends the original black-painted storage box beneath a blue hue.

The double candleholder in iron hanging above a reproduction wall box is another of Kathy Nugent's pieces.

Kari's large kitchen was built in place by Tim. The table in the center of the room is an old English pub table intended to be used as a skittle table. Skittle is a type of table bowling, and the top of this table lifts to expose the slate-lined playing field. Kari said no one wanted to be around as her husband tried to carry the piece up two flights of stairs!

*Kari's counters are soapstone, which she loves. She finds them maintenance-free, except that she applies mineral oil, which in a year's time has darkened the counters from a light gray similar to the cabinets to a charcoal gray.*

A small pantry off the kitchen was difficult to photograph because of its size. Beneath the wine rack, a small soapstone sink is barely visible.

A 19thC cheese safe holds a collection of yellowware. The churn to the left retains its original red wash. Kari has placed an early mustard bucket bench on the wall because, "She ran out of space on the floor."

The walls in the Cameron home were hand-palmed, meaning the plaster was applied to the dry wall with a bare hand. Kari used an ivory paint on her walls called "Burberry Beige". The 10-foot table was milled from 200 year-old pine support beams. The hunt board at the back is a reproduction. The portrait of a young man comes from an Alaskan estate.

A 19thC footed box, perhaps used to store documents, is stacked atop a small trunk. The Windsor chair is a reproduction.

The lift top chest with single wide board front dates to the mid-1700's. A dated 1838 sampler hangs above it.

The large armoire is a Wisconsin piece dated 1867; it was made to split apart and has a groove on top where a board runs through to keep the two pieces together.

An early gathering basket is filled with more greens and bright red berries.

Kari's son Tim made the wall shelf with delightful cutout skirt. The George Washington picture hanging above is a hand-painted portrait on tin.

Kari has draped a primitive long-necked goose with mixed greenery.

Kari's shop specializing in early antiques, pine tables, quilts, Windsor chairs, woven goods, upholstered furniture, wrought iron, redware, and accessories is open Monday - Saturday, 10-5. Please call for Sunday hours. Kari may be reached at 262-542-8050.

# Chapter 2

### ❧ ✽ ❧

## *Barbara and David English*

Barbara and David English of Rochester, Massachusetts, bought their large center chimney colonial 24 years ago. The house, built by Thomas Swift, dates to 1745 and features six working fireplaces.

Barbara, who has owned her country shop *The Gingham Goose* since 1987, clusters greens with pipe cleaners to create the effect of window boxes. She closes the windows, pulling the pipe cleaners inside as the greens are displayed outside. David has tried to retire a few times but becomes restless and goes back to a different job. Currently he is with Comcast. Neither David nor Barbara is ready to sell their home yet, but both look forward to owning a smaller, newer home on one floor.

A weathered birdhouse sits on the dry red painted bench on the porch.

The sitting room is decorated in soft tones of beige and gold with accents in the colorful large round rug.

The old Franklin stove is original to the house and holds a blue green painted box filled with fruits and greens. The mantel display consists of composition Belsnickels similar to those Barbara sells in her shop. Barbara purchased the oil on wood over the mantel at a consignment shop.

An early trencher in the center of the large table in front of the settee holds a collection of early pin cushions and wooden spools of thread.

The Windsor chairs in the dining room are new pieces from Ashland, which Barbara carries in her shop. The table is newly made from old boards.

A large stepback holds a collection of early yellowware and newer redware. David is a potter and Barbara is hoping that at some point he might be interested in making redware pieces.

On top of the stepback, a hand carved Noah's Ark with more carved animals than Barbara can count takes up the entire shelf. There isn't a species of animal missing from her collection, according to Barbara.

An early yarn winder hangs from the beam over the dining room fireplace. Lots of green boughs are draped between the manganese brown crocks and candleholders.

Vintage children's socks in shades of blue and gray are displayed on the quilt rack, where an early quilt is used as a backdrop.

The original kitchen was narrow and small so David and Barbara had it enlarged and beautifully remodeled.

The original well, shown above left, was incorporated into the kitchen area. Two primitive dolls, perhaps Humpty Dumptys, sit on the edge. The well is 40 feet deep, but David added an insert to prevent people and pets from falling in.

A small nook off the kitchen is a perfect spot for the reproduction bucket bench and hanging black cupboard.

Barbara used a coverlet similar to those she sells in her shop and draped it across the top of the bed. She then crimped the edges and fastened them to give the canopy a scalloped edge.

Tucked in the corner of the master bedroom, Barbara's latest rug hooking project is almost complete. A grouping of wicker at one end of the room allows for a quiet spot for reading.

Barbara has recently relocated her shop, The Gingham Goose, to a barn behind her home in Rochester. She can be reached by phone at 508-763-3018.

# Chapter 3

## *Cheryl and Bill Bonin*

Five years ago, Bill, an account executive with Coca-Cola, and Cheryl, a social worker, purchased a tavern in Sutton, Massachusetts. The tavern, built in 1775, witnessed a few additions during the 1800's, but essentially the front looks as it did almost 250 years ago. Cheryl became so interested in researching its history that she is now the President of the Historical Society. The tavern was first operated by Samuel Waters, who lived there with his wife Prudence. Cheryl learned that Samuel had a checkered past, as he apparently spent some time in debtor's prison resulting from a land deal gone bad. He must have seen the errors of his ways, however, as he then became a minister in town. Bill and Cheryl purchased the tavern from a man who was by trade a carpenter specializing in restoration of old homes. Over the 25 years he and his wife

lived in the house, he completed much of the home's restoration, as only the kitchen remained for Bill and Cheryl to remodel.

A barn in the back was used as a grist mill before it became the previous owner's workshop. It sits on top of a stream with a quiet waterfall at one end. Cheryl hopes one day to convert the barn into an antique shop.

Entering through the front door, a visitor enters Bill and Cheryl's living room, most likely the original tavern room. A maple drop leaf table holds a basket of greens and a Santa figure.

The built-in corner cupboard, original to the house, is filled with some of Cheryl's Vaillencourt folk art collection and chalk ware Santa figures.

*Cheryl found the early lift-top oxblood red painted desk, shown left, in Maine; she was on her way home and turned around to buy it. It rests on a red painted table base.*

*Cheryl had the new Waters Tavern sign made. A small tree sits in a stoneware crock on top of the desk.*

*Cheryl waited for over 10 minutes for a woman in front of her at an antique sale to decide she didn't want the standing dough box in red paint. Cheryl grabbed it immediately. Not only is the red base terrific, the top is hand planed with natural rich patina.*

Cheryl found the banister back chair dating to the 1700's in Maine. The tripod next to it is a primitive make-do candlestand with a tin candlestick attached to the tripod. Cheryl was thrilled to find the musket over the fireplace at Brimfield because the barrel is stamped "Waters". Cheryl has since found that the Waters family operated a gun manufacturing plant nearby.

An old barn lantern hangs on a hook above a stoneware crock with a small tree sparsely decorated with spice balls.

A blue gray painted cupboard next to the fireplace holds a large painted dough bowl on each shelf. The red and black gameboard on top is early.

Shown above, a red apothecary is another Brimfield find. The drawers and handles are large, leading Cheryl to think it might have come from a factory.

The bucket bench on the left holds lots of painted pantry boxes and a small feather tree on the top shelf in the mortar and pestle.

A tree in the corner of the dining room takes on a tavern theme with cards and tankards as decorations. Beneath the tree, early liquor bottles are arranged beside keg-like buckets draped with tobacco.

Cheryl found the original portraits of Samuel and Prudence Waters, painted by Winthrop Chandler, in a museum and was able to obtain high resolution digital renditions, which an artist attached to canvases. They now enjoy a place of honor over the Bonin's fireplace.

An early cupboard with salmon paint is dressed with a simple boxwood wreath. A carrier and early tavern bottle rest on top.

Early crocks are displayed on a drop leaf blue painted table. The wooden candlestand is early and was found in Brimfield. The tavern sign over the table is a new piece.

Cheryl and Bill had David T. Smith completely remodel their kitchen. Some of his redware can be seen displayed on the shelves. Cheryl's sink is soapstone.

Cheryl loves to collect scrub boards and early scouring boards; some of her collection is displayed in the corner. She also collects early butter presses and has grouped them on the shelves interspersed with a few greens and Santas.

Cheryl's refrigerator is hidden behind the large door and drawers.

The sideboard, shown above left, was originally created by David T. Smith as an island, but Cheryl could not get accustomed to not having a kitchen table; so the island quickly became a sideboard, and of course was immediately decorated with painted smalls!

Early pewter with great patina is seen on the mantel. An early hunt board in red holds baskets, bowls, and molds. An early brown tavern bottle sits on a small red stool in the parson's cupboard.

The master bedroom is huge and retains original painted florals throughout, as well as faux grain painting on the doors. The bottom panels are also painted. This room was originally used as the tavern's ballroom, and Cheryl has yet to determine if Samuel or one of his relatives painted the walls-perhaps in exchange for room and board. The walls are spectacular and unlike anything I've seen. Reportedly the previous owner was about to sell the house when he heard the prospective buyers say, "The first thing we're going to do is to paint the upstairs bedroom" – and he refused to sell them the house-which is listed in the National Register of Historical Places.

A small red painted bucket holds a country decorated tree in a salmon early painted dry sink.

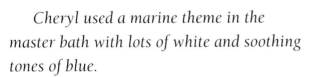

Cheryl used a marine theme in the master bath with lots of white and soothing tones of blue.

A shorebird sits in a small blue box on the vanity top and more birds are seen on the wall shelf over the blue chest in the corner. The tavern sign below is a new piece but uses the same blue tones.

# Chapter 4

─◦❤◦─

## Jane and Barron Hansen

When Barron and Jane Hansen decided to downsize two years ago, they were convinced they would never find a home they loved as much . . . until they stepped into this 1780 home in Holden, Massachusetts. They knew immediately that they would buy the house, as it felt like home from the start. Jane and Barron dated in high school, and while Barron wanted to marry, Jane admits she was independent and wasn't ready to settle down. They parted-with Barron telling Jane he pitied the man who married her. Their paths crossed occasionally through mutual friends, and 15 years later, Barron became the man he said he would pity! They've been happily married for 25 years. While Jane works as a part-time dental hygienist and Barron is a former manager with a communications company, their real passion is folk art and various Early American mediums. Be sure to note the last few pictures of this chapter and discover Jane's magnificent theorems and the Rufus Porter landscapes and tavern signs Barron paints.

Upon entering the side door, a visitor's eyes are immediately drawn to the large sunroom off the back of the house, which opens up from the kitchen. The sunroom was added 12 years ago.

The 19thC dry sink was purchased from the previous owners. Jane has filled the top with jugs, a fabric cat, a small tree, and a Belsnickel.

One of Barron's Rufus Porter style paintings is shown left. The reader may recognize the painting as it appeared on the cover of the Circa Home Living catalog.

The tree in the window, which stands on an old chest, is adorned with bronze-colored balls and gold resin pears. The tree's two-color scheme is striking in its simplicity and uniformity.

Barron made the table in front of the high camel back sofa. He also made the settle on the far side of the kitchen.

Jane enjoys decorating the original post in the center of the room. She admits that at one time she preferred a more contemporary style of decorating-and now can't tolerate "anything shiny". She has discovered that applying Caromal Colours Toner can age anything, as shown by the stocking hanging on the post. The toner affords her the opportunity to purchase inexpensive smalls and age them so they fit naturally into Barron and Jane's early decorating scheme.

Barron made the gameboard beside the entrance to the first floor bathroom, while Jane painted and aged the pantry boxes.

A small, cute bathroom features rough pine walls. The small windows are found in each room across the front of the house. Jane places a cordless candle in each window and faithfully lights each one daily, as she dislikes the look of hanging cords.

The kitchen is painted with a hue called "Salmon" from The Seraph. The sink is composite granite from Lowes.

Barron did the small portrait over the stove; it is heavily crackled to create an aged look.

Jane used toner on the small holiday sampler on the counter.

When I returned home I immediately placed two German sheep and brush trees on the sill over my sink as Jane has done. The mica adds a nice holiday touch.

The treen bread plate and mortar and pestle are old. Jane uses an LED candle in the tin sconces.

Beneath the stairway at the opposite end of the kitchen, an early woodbin with original dry red wash holds an old berry filled basket. The spoon rack above was purchased from Circa Home Living. The fireplace utensils beside the wood stove are early.

Jane also purchased the pewter spoons and small pewter plate from Circa Home Living.

Barron made the large farm table in the dining room from old boards. Six birdcage Windsor chairs surround the table; the end chairs are early and the other four reproductions.

The painting over the mantel is a reproduction that Jane applied with toner. The candlesticks are old sand-filled pieces. The Santa at the end is a folk art piece by Judi Vaillancourt.

A Marsh Homestead Country Antiques LED wax pillar stands in the middle of a faux Williamsburg wreath purchased in Sturbridge, Massachusetts.

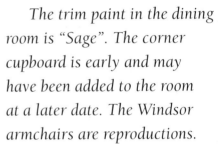

The trim paint in the dining room is "Sage". The corner cupboard is early and may have been added to the room at a later date. The Windsor armchairs are reproductions.

Jane and Barron found the two-door cabinet at The Christmas Tree Shop and knew its size and style was perfect. Barron used black antiquing glaze over Paprika Caromal Colours to achieve the old red finished surface; Barron added the reproduction rat tail hinges. The spoon rack above is new.

A built-in cupboard is filled with new redware pieces. Barron painted the Joshua Alden Tavern sign on an old bread board, which he deliberately split to create an aged look.

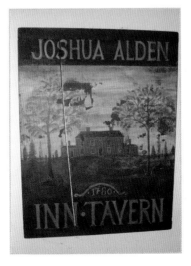

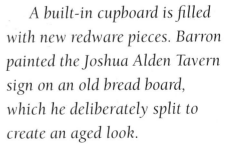

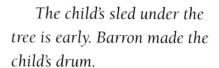

The child's sled under the tree is early. Barron made the child's drum.

Jane and Barron stenciled the walls in the formal parlor and then aged them with Ralph Lauren faux antiquing glaze. Barron purchased the tall cupboard in the corner at an unfinished furniture store and then painted it. The Martha Washington armchair was purchased at The Seraph. Barron made both the small sofa table and hanging plate rack. The camelback sofa with crewel upholstery is a Seraph piece.

The front door retains its original lock and latch. The demi-lune table was found at a tag sale and is approximately 50 years old.

I could look at this picture for hours! The theorem above the mantel is one of Jane's pieces. The colors and composition blend beautifully with the Williamsburg fruit arrangement on the mantel; the mustard trim paint pulls it all together.

The room off the parlor is where Jane and Barron spend the majority of their time. The trim paint is a deep colonial blue, while the upholstered furniture is mustard and black. Barron made the small bench from old boards.

A small tree hides in the corner, simply decorated with resin gingerbread boys, wooden stars, and a large tin star.

Barron made the mustard stepback cupboard from old boards to conceal a large flat screen television.

Tucked in the corner over the Windsor chair is one of Barron's Rufus Porter style landscapes.

Barron and Jane recently started their own business and can be reached through their website www.earlyamericanartists.com. To request a brochure of their pieces, email at barron.hansen@yahoo.com, or call 508-829-5307. In addition to the theorems on canvas, landscapes, and tavern signs, Barron paints homes from a photograph sent to him in the style or period of the homeowner's choice.

# Chapter 5

❖

## *Helen Brown*

Helen Brown has collected for over 40 years and attributes her initial interest in antiques to her brother-an auctioneer. He would describe to her the old pieces and what they sold for at auction. Helen had always dreamed of owning a shop; and with her husband Jess' blessing and support, Helen converted her Keeping Room to a shop

called *Corner House Antiques.* Helen operated the business from their home for four years until she and Jess built a cabin for the business in their hometown of Sutton, West Virginia.

Helen, now a widow, still enjoys collecting, and what she can't find, her son Todd creates. The only child of Helen's four who enjoys primitives is a talented craftsman who designs and builds pieces which he sells to shops and end users. Throughout the chapter you'll read, "Todd made that!"

Helen's circa 1906 home is a tribute to her son and her late husband who created many of her pieces. Jess took an active role in the shop and earned a reputation for restoring and repairing early pieces for customers. He also made all the tin lighting in their home.

A visitor can enter Helen's home at any time of the year and find her ready for the holidays, as she leaves her greens and a few holiday decorations up year 'round.

The coverlet draped over the camel back sofa in the living room is an early piece; it is not signed or dated but in mint condition. The primitive trunk, used as a coffee table, retains its original rope handles.

Todd made the large log folk art house as a gift to his mother. When I asked if it represented her home, Helen said, "It was the house she always dreamed of living in." It stands on an old cupboard which Helen's husband, Jess, adapted to accommodate the television.

A small artificial twig tree, purchased at Nanny's Primitives in Flatwoods, West Virginia, holds a collection of small tin ornaments. The old book leaning against the base is a Santa Claus book found in the house when they moved in. The sampler above is a reproduction.

A two-door cherry corner cupboard holds three large early baskets and is draped with a simple garland, a style Helen likes to use throughout her home.

The yarn winder is early and stands in front of a 19thC slatted ladderback chair. Todd made the standing candleholder, one of several styles Helen has displayed in the house.

A large church pew rests against the long wall on the other side of the room.

The shelf over the pew provides space to display Helen's pewter plates and textile samples. The shelf is one of Todd's creations and was a birthday gift to Helen.

Todd also painted the portrait over the mantel and made the wooden standing candlestand, seen above.

A hearthside early chair holds a vintage basket filled with ragballs. The small benches are early painted pieces.

I told Helen I could live in this room as its peacefulness is contagious. She replied that this is the room where she escapes to when she wants to shut out the modern world. This room previously housed Helen's shop.

Todd built the farm table, which Helen prefers over the early one she owned previously. A dried pineapple sits in the early trencher, which shows wonderful wear. Jess made the settle seen in the background for Helen. She marked the first one he made high enough in the shop, (she thought), no one would buy it. It sold immediately.

Helen repurposed an early hay hook as a rack to display candles and dried berries.Helen displays an early collection of hearthside iron pots. The tin candlebox in red was made by Todd. A vintage tin coffee grinder is tucked amongst the greens beside a stoneware crock.

Helen uses the bookcase beside the fireplace to hold her painted doughbowls. She has filled the old cloth sack with sawdust to resemble a sack of flour. The mustard pie safe is early and retains its original tins.

Another of Todd's table candleholders stands at the end of the table. Bunches of drieds hang above a candle drying rack made by Todd.

The chest on top of the stack is an old veterinary chest found in an old barn. The bottom chest is a small blanket box with dry blue paint.

Dried gourds fill the old sifter on the table.

Helen uses twig garlands draped over the top of the corner cupboard for a festive look. A few of Helen's belsnickels are seen on the shelves. Helen made the curtains and tacks them to create a casual draped appearance. A child's blue chair in robin's egg blue hangs on a peg rack beside the stairway leading upstairs. Helen used a paint from Wal-Mart called "Stonehedge" throughout the house, which takes on a different depth in each room depending on the light.

An old rake and farm tool are tucked in the corner behind an early barrel with red paint. Todd made the primitive red dry sink.

Helen purchased her large cherry pegged dining room table at a tag sale. She later discovered that the table came from the basement of the church where her mother and father were married. The wonderful blue cupboard was sitting in Helen's brother-in-law's garage when she asked if she could have it; he was happy to clean it up and "get rid of that old thing." A carpenter's tool carrier holds bowls and greens.

Dry painted smalls dress up the stepback in the corner. A large trencher of dried pomegranates stands on the bottom shelf.

The chalky white candlestick is another of Todd's pieces. The make-do chair was made by Todd as a gift.

The single hanging garland on the early corner cupboard creates a simple country look.

The far corner is the perfect spot for the 19thC small pie safe which Helen traded a flat wall cupboard for. Three large early stoneware crocks fit nicely under the reproduction mustard painted shelf.

The 19thC candlemold hanging beside a small swing-handled basket was a gift from Helen's husband on their 49th wedding anniversary. A tiny sprig of greens and a carved bird adorn the small wall cupboard.

Helen refers to this room as her old kitchen. The old pantry, seen at the end of the hall, is now her 2nd kitchen where she keeps her modern appliances and utensils.

The cupboard seen in the corner was made from old barnwood.

Todd made the hanging lantern in the window which looks out on the back porch. Note the lovely blue painted dough bowl on the table.

Helen filled the white dry sink with a crock holding a collection of early wooden spoons and a carrier filled with vintage cookie cutters.

Dry painted sap buckets and an early butter paddle are seen on the shelf in the left hand side of the picture.

I love Todd's sawbuck table which rests under the window. The corner cupboard at the end holds more of Helen's stoneware collection.

A peek into the old pantry shows Helen's working kitchen complete with yellowware and canned goods.

A crock holds a collection of early darning tools.

*A primitive portrait done by Todd hangs over the Jenny Lind bed in one of the guest rooms.*

*Helen's husband made the slant top desk seen below right.*

*Helen's grandchildren enjoy sleeping on the high rope bed with red paint when they come to visit.*

An early ladderback in one corner holds a large basket of ragballs while a sampling of early textiles hangs on a pegrack in the opposite corner. Helen calls this room the little boy's room. The bed is an early rope bed.

A pair of vintage child's shoes and boots rest on the blanket. Helen has placed a collection of vintage toys on the shelf above and in the wooden wagon beside the bed.

Three sap buckets stand in a dry sink made by Todd in the entranceway. A pair of high women's shoes hangs with early textiles above it.

Helen's back porch is filled with primitive treasures.

A shelf in the corner holds a collection of vintage tools. Below, a large chalk white bee skep sits in a twig chair.

Anyone wishing to reach Todd Brown may contact him at 304-534-4455.

# Chapter 6

❧ ✿ ❧

## *Pat and Chuck Knapp*

Many readers have asked if I would include a condominium and I'm pleased to present that of Pat and Chuck Knapp of Ohio. Former owners of the *Village Idiot Antique Shop* and now both retired, Pat and Chuck demonstrate that country decorating doesn't require a 250 year-old colonial to work its magic. Chuck and Pat sold their nearby early farmhouse and downsized in 2007. Pat finds that the only drawback is that with limited space, she must be more careful that what she buys will fit. Her shop, which she owned for 25 years, was based on the philosophy of carrying pieces which she would keep in her own home. She combined primitive antiques with contemporary folk art, like that created by Norma and Jennifer Schneeman. Pat prefers early paint but tastefully mixes attic surface and reproduction accessories.

The portrait over the sofa in the living room was purchased at auction. Pat and Chuck were drawn to the sitter despite the fact that, according to Pat, she looks as though she never missed a meal. The small settee fashioned from an early rope bed was made by Lori McClintock of The Added Touch.

A lovely 19thC corner cupboard with blue paint holds a selection of early textiles. On top sits a huge early redware bowl. A folk art Santa figure rests atop an early dapple child's rocking horse. The tavern sign was painted by Peter DiScala of Pennsylvania.

Seen against the back wall, a 19thC sink with original red wash is filled with greens. The sink retains its original wooden drain and is signed.

The grain-painted stepback cupboard in red and black is early 19thC. Pat displays stacked measures, pantry boxes, and sugar buckets on top. The box bottom left is constructed with rosehead nails and bands going in different directions. It is very possibly Shaker. Some of Chuck and Pat's collection of burl bowls fill the shelves.

A collection of Buffalo Pottery Santa figures mixes with early brush trees and greens on top of the 19thC jelly cupboard in the hallway. An early oil of an English setter hangs above it.

Pat collects unglazed redware, some of which she displays above the draped window.

The Pennsylvania table dates to the 19thC. The wall box above the child's chair was made by The Keeping Room in Galion, Ohio; the box conceals an electric switch. The rabbit sitting in the chair was crafted by Lori Baker of Ohio.

The wall shelf was made by Kathy Graybill of Hidden Treasures in Pennsylvania.

Pat uses the base of an early child's doll carriage to hold greens and a snowman as her table centerpiece.

On the wall beside the early Pennsylvania corner cupboard hangs a biscuit break found in Maryland. Pat learned after reading "What America Eats", by William Boys Weaver, that when bread was baked in the late 18thC and early 19thC, the cook could either beat the dough 500 times with an ax or use a biscuit break.

Greens and redware in a dry blue painted carrier sit on the island table.

Pat and Chuck purchased the mirror made from an early window frame at The Gleaner in Ashland, Ohio.

Pat has draped the lights with magnolia leaves. A Schneeman giraffe holds a light in its mouth on the left side of the picture.

Chuck and Pat's master bedroom is done in accents of gray and black. A large Noah's Ark fills the top of a bureau. Pat has placed wreaths on the front posts of the pineapple bed. A large Santa sits atop a tall chest of drawers in the back of the picture.

Pat enjoys rug hooking, but particularly cooking and baking bread. Now that Pat has retired, she finds time to write the book her customers encouraged her to write "The Village Idiot Cookbook". It will include many of the recipes Pat used when she held country luncheons at the farm house Pat and Chuck previously owned.

# Chapter 7

✦ ❋ ✦

## *Faith and Bill Moss*

Faith and Bill Moss like to keep their decorating style within the early 1800's, but still enjoy living in a 20 year old home, with, as Faith says, "straight walls and straight floors." After retiring from raising feeder pigs and 15,000 caged layers, Faith and Bill moved "down the road", where they have lived for 12 years. Faith worked in the antique business for 40 years, doing shows and maintaining space at an antique mall. She still has a large quantity of inventory and enjoys decorating and redecorating. Her favorites are painted New England pieces. She also enjoys painting shorebirds.

*A settee on the front porch was made from sassafras branches.*

*A small table holds a collection of handmade birdhouses. The grazing sheep were a gift to Faith from her daughter.*

Faith solved the problem of a home without a fireplace by purchasing a mantel from an early Indiana home. A friend painted the fireboard and Faith used old bricks to create the hearth.

The full-bodied shorebird on the hearth features iron legs and is signed. The 19thC spinning wheel retains its original dark red paint. The portrait above the mantel was purchased at an Ohio auction.

The table with cutout corners is early. A sugar cone and nippers rest on top beside a pewter tea set.

Greens and magnolia leaves drape over the candleholder above the table. Faith loves early dough bowls; this large beehive bowl in red holds greenery and pomegranates for color. The round table is early and came from a log house in southern Tennessee; it retains its early attic gray painted base.

Faith found the 19thC grain bin and had a friend paint it, adding the scene at the bottom in a Rufus Porter style.

Another friend painted the picture above the bin and Faith purchased the old door from Olde Glory in Waynesville, Ohio, especially to display her friend's painting.

The gameboard is an early mustard and black painted folding board. Faith uses a standing apothecary with blue paint as a base to display one of her feather trees and a collection of belsnickels. Some of the belsnickels were carved by Jerry Bolinger, an art teacher from nearby North Manchester. An early child's sled can be seen at the edge of the picture; it retains its original red and green paint and the depiction of a horse's head.

Faith has over 200 early trenchers and dough bowls in her collection! The large one on top is most likely European and the smallest of a graduated set of three.

Bill made the red stepback which Faith designed and painted. Faith placed some of her shorebird collection on top with three of her favorite salt-glazed crocks.

Faith is holding the large settee in the entranceway for her daughter while a room in her home is completed. The early quilt is one of many in Faith's collection. A blue painted bench is tucked under the settee. A collection of gathering and buttocks baskets hangs from a beam above.

A large swan made by the Amish of Shipshewana, Indiana rests among greens on top of an early sawbuck table in the Keeping Room. The table, with original red paint, is unique in that a large drawer at each end extends to the opposite end of the table. The blue cupboard in the back is a Sally Whims. The large early mustard cupboard displays some of Faith's Schooner redware, which she has collected for over 20 years. Bill made the bowl rack which holds more of Faith's treen collection.

Faith displays two more of her early feather trees on a large cricket bench in original red paint.

A wonderful 19thC child's wagon in mustard paint with original wooden wheels holds another tree in the corner.

# Chapter 8

## ⌒ ✳ ⌒

# *Linda and Bruce McLaughlin*

Linda and Bruce McLaughlin have lived in their 1960's ranch-style home in Maine for over 25 years; with the use of historic colors and early pieces, they have created a 19C interior. When Linda started collecting 40 years ago, she began with maple pieces and has gradually updated to authentic antiques, preferring the early 19thC. Now retired from a large market research company, Linda also operated a small antique business for years. Her antique business brought her to many local auctions and in contact with collectors around the state. Now Linda enjoys collecting for her home and admits that good auctions are harder to find. When not out hunting, Linda enjoys rug hooking. In the summer, her garden keeps her busy canning produce, while the Maine snows find her out on the cross-country trails. On her favorite winter days she is snowed in and sitting in front of the fireplace.

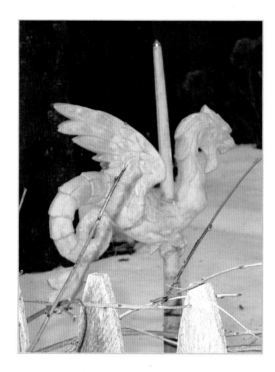

An early weathervane, styled after the Loch Ness monster, resembles an ice sculpture in the Maine snow.

A late 1700's tavern table stands between two wing back chairs in front of the large living room window. Part of a putz village consisting of trees, horses, and fence is displayed on the table beside an early platform horse child's pull toy.

The highboy, purchased at a Skinner auction in Boston, was one of the first pieces Linda and Bruce purchased and is one of Linda's favorites. At the time, she felt she paid an exorbitant amount for the piece but now recognizes that she wouldn't sell it for what she paid.

A French hat form stands in front of a Maine sampler dated 1840. The sampler depicts an armed man hiding behind a tree and a deer and rabbit in the distance.

I love the mustard-painted early bucket and the colors of the stone fruit; the vignette works well with the mustard-painted tin lamp. The 18thC table features an interesting chamfered center board. A portrait of a gentleman holding a dog hangs above the table and is the mate to the large portrait over the couch in the living room.

Linda used Old Village paint "Valley Forge Mustard" on the fireplace wall. Linda tried to involve Bruce in her antiques; since he enjoys bird hunting, she thought he might enjoy collecting vintage decoys. In the end, Linda put together the collection which is seen in part beside the fireplace.

The two pieces seen on the top shelf are a perfectly matched pair of canvas geese.

The tall cherry clock dates to the early 1800's and was made in Bridgeton, Maine; it features a window in front to display the workings.

The watercolors are English and from the "puffy-sleeved" era with unusual orange backgrounds. The frames are grain-painted.

A wooden compote holds more of Linda's stone fruit collection. The samplers over the camel back couch are two of 20 Linda owns. The sampler on the left is Scottish and depicts a sailing ship, while on the right is a dated 1866 Adam and Eve sampler. The large size of the portrait necessitated hanging it separately from the sitter's husband. His portrait hangs over the table holding the mustard bucket and stone fruit.

Linda painted the floor cloth with diamonds of dark green and red. A canted apple tray in dry red paint holds greens and pomegranates on the center of the table. The hutch table is pine and has two drawers on the far side. The reproduction pewter cupboard is a DR Dimes piece; Linda loves its lines and the amount of early pewter pieces it can accommodate. Linda's grandfather once worked at an inn called the Harrington House in New Hampshire transporting passengers who arrived by ship. Her grandfather inherited the birdcage Windsor chairs in the 1930's which her grandmother eventually sold. Linda was able to purchase them through a dealer so that they are now back in the family. A scrap of paper found beneath one chair tells of the Harrington House.

Linda purchased the Pennsylvania dry sink from an estate in Florida; stone fruit, greens, and an early box containing pomegranates adorn its shelves. The authentic wedding band candlesticks date to the 19thC.

Linda carried the "Valley Forge Mustard" paint into the kitchen. An early round treen board rests behind two treen containers; one holds kitchen utensils, the other Linda uses for sugar.

Linda displays a group of pears made of painted canvas from an early hanging scale.

Linda had the early maple canopy bed converted from a full to queen. The coverlet on the bed dates to 1861 while the folded coverlet is 1839.

Linda has placed two vintage belsnickels on the corner shelf along with wooly stick-legged sheep.

Tucked in the corner, a 19thC chest features graduated drawers and retains its original surface. Some of Linda's extensive toleware collection is displayed on top.

Linda couldn't resist the arched interior and fluted columns on the sides of the corner cupboard, which retains its original red wash. The panels are all hand-cut. Interestingly, the row of panels on the bottom opens down.

# Chapter 9

# *Susan and Tom Morello*

Sue Morello's home, Sheldon Farms, is surrounded by 75 acres of orchards, pine trees, and raspberry bushes. Tom and Sue purchased the 1753 house in 1994 and Sue has been restoring it ever since. They built an addition to the second floor in the back when they moved in. Currently Tom and Sue are in the process of building a three-season room off the deck and a cage bar in the dining room.

The transom was outfitted with custom bull's eye glass. The onion light is from *Hammer Works* in Worcester, Massachusetts. The labrador guards the front door in memory of their beloved black lab that passed away two years ago.

The formal living room at the front of the house opens to a stone patio. The couches come from Angel House in nearby Brookfield.

A friend of Sue's, Jody Cederlund Norris, created the hand-carved carolers displayed on a 19thC pine blanket chest. The Shaker clock is a reproduction.

The corner cupboard houses pottery from Old Sturbridge Village and a local potter. Sue found the large painted Santa, standing guard by the window, at a local shop. A folksy, whimsical Santa riding an ear of corn is displayed on top of the cupboard; this Santa was carved by Michele Wronsky.

*Sue used Old Sturbridge Village paint Fenno House Green in the livingroom. The angel above the fireplace was carved by local artisan David Small. The mirrored round sconces are period pieces found at Brimfield. The reproduction settle seen in front of the mural, painted by a local artist, is a new piece purchased at The Seraph in Sturbridge, MA.*

A bed warmer rests beside a green reproduction jelly cupboard. A pewter plate and set of graduated pewter measures nestle among the greens.

An old oil lamp holds red berries picked on the property. The Santa carving was done by Jody Cederland Norris.

At the end of the dining room at the back of the house rests a large fresh-cut tree picked from many on the property. An old rocking horse sits in front.

The tree is filled with unique ornaments collected over the years; many are handmade, and each has a special memory.

Sue dresses the crow, carved by Ken Graves, for each season. He sits in a large wooden trencher in the center of the dining room table.

A cupboard in the corner conceals the television. Sue purchased the carved Santa figures from an artist she found on the Internet.

Sue found the old red shelf at Brimfield; it holds a collection of old books, a teddy bear, and a few old toys. Sue keeps an extensive collection of antique teddy bears; one of her favorites, seen left, sits on an old settle and holds a pillow with a Christmas greeting.

Another bear, seen left, sits among some of Sue's early candlemold collection on an old mustard corner cupboard.

Sue maintains a Website, created by her son as a gift, where she sells her handmade baskets. For more information, contact Sue through her Website www.sheldonfarmbaskets.com.

# Chapter 10

❖ ⊛ ❖

## *Michelle and Donny Logan*

Michelle and Donny Logan built their saltbox colonial 12 years ago on three acres of open Pennsylvania land. A winding driveway leads to the house nestled at the base of a hill. Every window features a magnificent view of distant mountains and open spaces. Michelle's dad is a contractor and was able to do all the restoration; care was taken to use old wood and replicate an authentic 19thC home. Michelle owns a shop in nearby Reedsville, Pennsylvania, called *Squire Brown's.*

Weathered shingles and bright red painted trim highlight the lines of the Logan's replica saltbox colonial and garage. Large holly bushes surround the front door, while a full wreath of mixed greens and red berries welcomes holiday visitors.

Michelle has dressed the side entrance with the same type of greens. An early child's sled rests beside the door while a huge basket of greens completes the vignette.

The Logans used authentic old bricks in their front hall entrance. Tucked in the corner is an early hutch table with a 19thC coverlet draped over the back.

An early crock holds fresh cut greens. Hanging on the corner of the hutch table, a leather band of early jingle bells adds a holiday flare. A simple early basket hangs on the wall.

Signed frakturs by Suasn Daul hang above an early walnut drop leaf table. A vintage German feather tree with a flock of small German sheep rests at one end.

Michelle leaves the Williamsburg-style spray of dried greens and eucalyptus on the raised panel mantel in the living room up all year. A small table with turned legs holds an early document box and brass candlestick. The mirror on the wall is similar to those Michelle sells in her shop.

The clock in the corner dating to the 1900's is from Pennsylvania.

A candlestand holds a poinsettia plant, while a walnut Sheridan drop front desk can be seen in the background. The Windsor bow back chair is early.

Vintage silhouettes are clustered over the desk. An early Staffordshire plate can be seen beside another small poinsettia.

Michelle uses a pitcher filled with a bouquet of greenery to dress up her dining room farm table; the table dates to the 19thC and features a three-board top. The chairs are from DR Dimes. The Chippendale mirror hanging beside the walnut and cherry corner cupboard retains its original glass.

A three-foot German feather tree sits on the side table beside the wingback chair in the corner. The portraits of Mr. and Mrs. Pierce are reproductions.

Garlands of pine and holly dress the Pennsylvania Dutch cupboard filled with early pewter.

The Keeping Room extends across the entire back of the house. A six-board chest in early red with turned feet holds a large pewter bowl of greens and fruit.

Additional pieces of pewter are displayed over the simple mantel. A stocking filled with greens can be seen at one end.

A half-round table in pine with an early red wash base fits perfectly under the molding alongside the stairs. An early German feather tree is decorated with old cotton batting fruit.

At the corner of the stair landing, a salt glazed jug and large cobalt decorated pitcher hold more greens.

A large primitive cupboard in old red paint is filled with greens and wonderful handmade Santas fashioned by an artisan from Ohio.

Two small oval Harvard boxes are shown on the middle shelf. A small stack of folded holiday green and red fabric sits on the bottom shelf.

Michelle's countertops are pine, as is the counter shelf over the island. Michelle wanted her cupboards to look like furniture, so her dad added legs to simulate standing cabinets. Michelle's sink is soapstone. The redware plate resting on the deep windowsill with drawers was made by David T. Smith.

Stacks of attic surface and painted pantry boxes and a firkin cluster under the hanging cupboard beside a large lidded cake crock with cobalt blue glaze. An early large apothecary fits perfectly under the cupboard. Some of Michelle's pottery collection is displayed on top.

Michelle has placed a simple poinsettia on the dresser in the master bedroom. The cotton coverlet is accented with navy blue toile bed skirt and shams.

In the corner of the master bedroom, an early schoolmaster's desk holds simple greens, an early pewter inkwell, and two silhouettes.

The mirror over the chest of drawers is a new piece. An early box with drawers rests on top of the chest.

Vintage clothing and an early shoe form hang from a peg rack which surrounds the room. What a great way to add additional display space!

Michelle maintains a Website for her shop, www.squirebrowns.com, where her location and hours of operation are available.

# Chapter 11

❧ ✿ ❧

## *Sue and Chris Wendt*

Sue, a pre-kindergarten teacher, and I first met about 10 years ago through ebay. I was selling early painted pieces at the time and Sue was one of my customers. In fact, I first met Chris, Sue's husband, on the Cross Bronx Expressway in New York City after agreeing to deliver an early cupboard. As I filmed Sue and Chris' house, I recognized many pieces and felt a twinge of regret that I had sold them in the first place! Sue has collected for years and recalls when she was 12, her mother brought her to Colonial Williamsburg, a visit which sparked her interest and love of antiques. Sue and Chris live in the house where she grew up, and Sue feels fortunate to have inherited some of the pieces in the house.

A crafted Santa, made by Alta's Heirlooms, rests on the right side of the mantel. A small tree is tucked in the corner and stands on one of Sue's five standing dough boxes.

A gorgeous blue 19thC six-board chest serves as the coffee table in the Keeping Room, while a dough box has been repurposed as an end table.

Sue made the portraits from prints. The bowl rack, a gift from Chris, holds redware plates depicting pineapples; Sue's extensive collection of pineapples can be seen throughout the house.

Sue made the Colonial Williamsburg-style board hanging over the 19thC pine ogee mirror in the hallway.

A large poinsettia stands in a stoneware crock on the table. The two Windsor chairs are reproductions.

The lovely New England pine chest, purchased by Sue's mother and seen right, holds a pewter pitcher; note the width of the single-board front. Sue often frequents a local thrift shop and found the pewter candlestick for $1.

Sue made the cross stitch seen above and displayed on the wall above the chest; I like Sue's unique use of color in the piece.

Each time I see the two-door blue painted cupboard seen in the picture right, I ask myself, "What was I thinking when I sold that piece?!" (Sue refuses to sell it back!). The maple table and chairs in the dining room belonged to Sue's parents.

Sue's mother owned the chest holding the Williamsburg style apple cone. Sue had a craftsman in Pennsylvania make the matching hanging cupboard on top to provide more display space.

Sue made the floor cloth which she uses as a center tablecloth.

Sue decorates a feather tree in the corner with small pineapples and other fruit; a plain white dove rests on top. The reproduction spoon rack holds antique pewter spoons.

Belsnickels and sheep are displayed on the blue stepback in the corner.

A small red hanging cupboard holds a collection of Santas and a small plate that Sue used as a child.

A standing dough box is tucked in the corner of the dining area of the kitchen. Sue uses an early child's quilt as a center tablecloth. A weathered blue painted shutter holds a holiday wreath and hangs beside a large wooden pineapple.

Sue carries a blue theme throughout the house; the blue coverlet blends beautifully with the folded textile at the foot of the bed.

Sue did the red work on the pillow shams. The rug hanging on the wall was purchased from The Country House in Maryland.

Sue and Chris hope to move to St. Augustine, Florida, where they have often vacationed. Sue particularly enjoys St. Augustine, not only because it is the oldest city in the United States, but because of its Spanish and British history and the blending of early American pieces used in the restored areas of the city.

# Chapter 12

  ❖  

## *Priscilla and Pete Mathieus*

Priscilla and Pete Mathieus of Norwichtown, Connecticut, have lived in their 1970's cape for eight years. I think the color of the house gives the house an older look, and I asked Priscilla what paint they used. She replied that the house is painted with "Valley Forge Mustard" from Old Village, while the trim is "British Red", also from Old Village.

When they moved in, the house was well-kept, but Pete and Priscilla immediately went to work remodeling the kitchen and making cosmetic changes in keeping with their country décor.

Priscilla loves to garden and plans to leave the fence around the front of the house. In the spring, the plan is to remove the raised beds and replace them with grass, and perhaps a cherry tree. As with many of us, she is looking to simplify and make life easier. Priscilla has placed two artificial trees topped with a bird in each of her flower boxes at the front windows.

An entranceway into the kitchen holds a large 19thC red wash cupboard with wonderful shelves for extra storage. Three painted measures nestle in greens on top.

The Mathieus' kitchen is done with an Olde Century paint called "Thistle", which at times takes on a tan hue and other times a soft gray tone. Pete and Priscilla replaced their cupboards with Shaker style cupboards. Priscilla reports that she is pleased with her maple countertops.

Early tin lidded jars cluster in the corner. Priscilla has a passion for apothecaries and other small cupboards which can be seen throughout the house.

An island holds a small German feather tree, a compote bowl of stone fruit, and a spiced wax lamb made by Marsh Homestead Country Antiques.

A large single-board jelly cupboard stands next to a smaller wall cupboard which houses the telephone. Baskets, greenery, early measures, and a small hooked Santa decorate two wall cupboards between the kitchen and eating areas.

The large 19thC open cupboard was a find at a Walker Homestead show; it hangs over a table made from old boards and a new green painted base. The red jelly cupboard at the end holds different colored cutlery boxes on each shelf.

A tiny dry gray painted wall cupboard hangs to the left of the jelly cupboard. Priscilla has placed a miniature striped stocking filled with greens on the door.

The large living room off the kitchen area was streaked with light when I visited, spotlighting the soft greens with red and mustard accents. The red table in the center of the room is from the Maynard House in Massachusetts. The hooked rug on top is a new piece. The large cupboard in the corner holds a television.

Priscilla found the oil portrait over the mantel in the Berkshires. The Windsor chair in front of the fireplace is one of DR Dimes' earliest Windsors.

Tucked in the corner behind the flame-stitched wing chair, a small single-drawer table in red holds an early red box. The 19thC sampler above is signed. The wall box in paint features a single drawer and holds small leather books. A few sprays of pine dress the early child's sled leaning against the mantel.

The primitive cupboard over the couch shows evidence of many layers of paint; but what a great look; a small ring of greens is just enough to set it off. Three early baskets, one of them Native American, rest alongside a few sprigs of green.

A pine stepback is filled with early redware. The decoy, nesting in the greens on top, is early.

An early red apothecary purchased from Betty Urqhardt stands to the left of the mantel and holds a small wooden box filled with a small feather tree and a newer Belsnickel.

In the front hall, a short stack of painted boxes blends with the mural done by Sue Dwyer of Rhode Island.

The sitting room at the front of the house is trimmed in blue, accenting the shades of soft tans, blues, and reds throughout the room. Priscilla found the patterned rug on QVC! It matches beautifully with the antique chenille fabric covered loveseats. The early table was purchased at Louise Villa's The Bowl Barn in Douglas, Massachusetts.

The portrait seen left, hanging over an early red cupboard with a wide single-board door, was found at Brimfield. A small ring of greens hangs on the knob. An early Windsor in the corner is tucked under a small painted cupboard filled with leather books.

Priscilla found the early red blanket chest in New England. An early signed sampler hangs on the wall above a painted document box and stack of painted pantry boxes.

The early black candlestand, which holds a leather book and leather glasses case, was purchased from Wirth Antiques in Connecticut.

The cupboard in the corner is a newly made piece from old wood, while an assortment of ovoid shaped jugs fills the shelves.

A Santa figure carrying a small feather tree rests on the lift-top chest. Above, a pastoral oil depicting a red cape reminds Priscilla of their home. The schoolmaster's desk in red paint is a Brimfield find.

The table and chairs in the formal dining room are new pieces which Priscilla hopes to replace some day.

A collection of dough bowls with early paint is arranged on the table.

Old pewter measures, teapots, and plates line the shelves of the green painted stepback. An early stamped basket sits on top while five blue and green firkins are stacked alongside.

As I photographed the beautiful two-door jelly cupboard, I suddenly realized that it looked familiar and must have come from Virginia – since I remembered to whom I had sold it; Priscilla confirmed that it was indeed the same cupboard.

Above the red dry sink filled with painted dough bowls, a small wooden shelf holds a collection of Pease ware. Priscilla loves the color and texture of the lidded wooden pieces and has managed to collect seven. Leather books are another of Priscilla's passions.

A large tree is decorated with an assortment of new and old ornamental birds. Alongside, a chest holds a collection of graduated stoneware.

The large apothecary was found in Massachusetts and appears to be a built-in, as it is missing a back. A collection of mortar and pestles rests on top. Hanging above, an early red candlebox holds greens and five small chalkware Belsnickels

Priscilla decorated the small bath off the kitchen with small early boxes filled with diminutive baskets and leather books.

A 19thC dry sink holds a vessel sink and small feather tree.

A pair of simple mittens adds holiday flair to the small cupboard over the commode.

A hanging wall box with red wash was found at Nancy Bryer's in Colchester, Connecticut.

A porch off the kitchen provides an ideal spot for summer dining. A standing sorting tray holds a feather tree and lidded red bucket.

The entire house is beautifully decorated and makes clear that Priscilla's hobby is her home. She enjoys stenciling and decorating and, of course, the hunt for antiques. Priscilla admits that, like many of us, she experiences withdrawal when she's not been out on the antiquing trail for a while.

# Chapter 13

# *Karen and Michael Casey*

Karen and Michael Casey built their colonial home in Massachusetts 25 years ago when, as Karen says, "before they knew what they know now." Anxious to return to the town where Karen grew up, they sold the small cape they purchased when first married, hired an architect, and built their new house on land formerly owned by the Draper Corporation. The Caseys discovered a great deal of bones when excavating and have since learned that their house is built on land previously used as a pig farm.

The color of the house is a Benjamin Moore "doctored and altered" paint which Karen says doesn't have a name. The trim color is "Black Forest" by Benjamin Moore.

An early painted white basket holds fresh greens and red berries between the garage doors.

The sawbuck table in the center of the large Keeping Room was purchased at The Maynard House. The chairs are old and were purchased at Brimfield. The cupboard in the back was built by Jeff Dana of Western Massachusetts. The shelves are filled with baskets and bowls while a large basket on the top shelf holds dried herbs.

An early painted white bucket provides a nesting spot for a large gingerbread boy and greenery.

Although it looks like a single piece, the two red settles back to back create a "hallway" from the end of the Keeping Room into the front Gathering Room. It also provides an ideal spot to display some of Karen's collection of crocks and pitchers.

An early dough box with attic surface sits on the wide sill in the Keeping Room. A red bench, found at The Bowl Barn in Douglas, Massachusetts, sits beneath the window.

Karen found the candy cane striped candles at Country Plus in Hopkinton, Massachusetts.

A large winnowing board rests against the wall behind another large gingerbread boy. Baskets hang from the beam while an early peel hangs on the wall above a stack of measures.

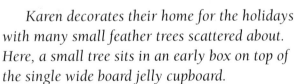

Karen decorates their home for the holidays with many small feather trees scattered about. Here, a small tree sits in an early box on top of the single wide board jelly cupboard.

When Michael and Karen first built their home, the kitchen was open and located at one end of the Keeping Room. Karen decided 10 years later that she preferred the kitchen as an enclosed area. She added a cage bar which accomplished her goal of separating the kitchen area, while at the same time creating a bright, open room.

Henry waits patiently for me to leave so he can have his supper.

Karen used a small measure to hold this tiny tree on the counter of the cage bar.

A make-do spoon rack hangs on the side of the jelly cupboard in red paint. A bucket bench in gray holds a red bucket filled with greens.

A friend's husband made the small cabinet in the first floor bath. Because of the small size of the vanity, Karen purchased a copper bar sink which fits perfectly.

Karen purchased the small sawbuck table from Nancy Bryer in Connecticut. The corner cabinet holds the television and is a new piece. The mule chest in red is from New England. A reproduction hunt board with hooks holds dried herbs and a rod of candles.

A small wall cupboard in blue paint was found at The Bowl Barn in Douglas, Massachusetts.

A vintage red bucket holds a small tree decorated with fabric hearts and stars. A small handmade angel acts as the tree topper. The blue painted chest was found locally.

Early boxes with attic surface are shown on the shelves of the open stepback pine cupboard.

The table in the dining room is new, as are the chairs. The floor cloth is hand-painted and was purchased at The Keeping Room in Douglas.

A corner cabinet in blue contains early Beaumont Pottery.

A stoneware crock holds another small tree with seed lights on the sill in the dining room.

Redware plates and molds fill the large reproduction cupboard on the back wall.

Early painted buckets line up on the gray painted bucket bench under a rack draped with garlands.

Karen uses a wreath with pomegranates to encircle the vintage Paul Revere lantern at the center of the table.

A smaller Gathering Room at the back of the house is decorated in tones of sage and burgundy. A small tree in a bucket is seen on the end table next to the six-board early red chest. Karen again uses a wreath as a wonderful means to dress a lantern on the 19thC chest in gray paint.

In addition to placing small trees around their home, Karen also uses pineapples scattered about in bowls and on shelves.

Because Michael travels a great deal, he encourages Karen to pursue her interest and passion for collecting antiques. How envious are we?! During warm weather, Michael and Karen spend most of their time in their enclosed porch off the back. Another tree with seed lights rests on an early grain bin in the corner. The white hanging cupboard under the dried herbs was purchased at a local antique shop.

Karen has decorated her front hall in a patriotic theme. An Adirondack basket is filled with fresh greens on the stairway wall.

Karen has lined a beam in the stairwell with pond boats, one of which she found at The Christmas Tree Shop years ago for $10.

Karen enjoys living in an area rich with country shops and friends who enjoy collecting and sharing. When not working as a Medical Administrative Assistant, Karen can be found "making the rounds" of antique malls, shops and shows.

As I have mentioned, each book from start to finish takes 18-24 months. For that reason I'm usually working on a book at a different season of the year. The temperature could be 90 degrees when I'm writing a holiday book or 20 degrees when I'm writing about country gardens!

The final book in 2011 is entitled *A Touch of Country* and will be available late autumn. Work is underway for five books to be available in 2012. The first, *Back Home*, will feature Jeff's and my 'new' 1825 Massachusetts cape. Over 60 homes have been photographed for presentation in 2012, with another holiday book ready in September. As always, I welcome comments and suggestions so that I can better meet the needs of those of us who thrive on country decorating.

Although the temperature is currently over 90 degrees, I want to wish each of you happy holidays and best wishes for a prosperous and healthy New Year.

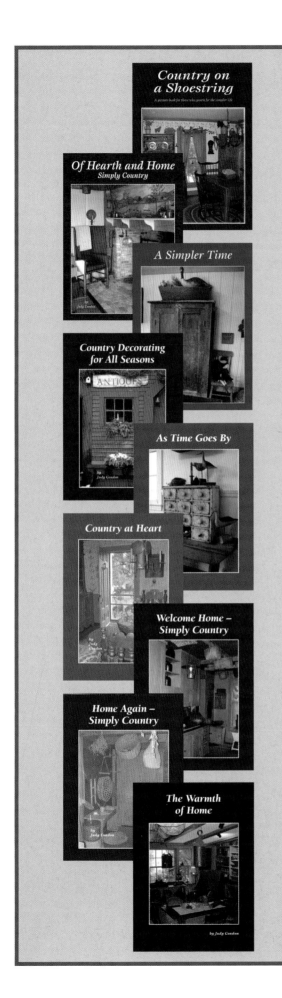

# The "simply country" book series

## by Judy Condon

### Country on a Shoestring
- 33 tips on how to decorate on a shoestring

### Of Hearth and Home
- mantels, old painted pieces, signs and primitives

### A Simpler Time
- log homes, bedrooms, kitchens, dining rooms, folk art and stencils

### Country Decorating for All Seasons
- holiday doors, porches, mantels, trees, vignettes; summer gardens, and fall decorating

### As Time Goes By
- The Keeping Room; boxes, baskets and bowls; The Privy; Hallways and Small Ways; The Guest Room

### Country at Heart
- The Tavern Room; early looms, dolls and bears; The Gathering Room; a kitchen aged to perfection; country gardens

### Welcome Home
- Over 350 photographs from 2 Connecticut homes and 5 Ohio homes.

### Home Again
- A house tour book featuring 1 Maine home and 7 Ohio homes including a never before photographed Shaker collection.

### The Warmth of Home
- 3 Massachusetts homes, 1 Pennsylvania home, 3 Ohio homes, 1 New York home and 1 Delaware home

# The "simply country" book series (cont'd)

### The Country Home
- 6 Ohio homes, 2 Massachusetts homes, and 1 New Hampshire home

### The Comfort of Home
- Over 325 color photographs showing a Massachusetts and Ohio home of two exceptional collectors. A Maine home; three Massachusetts homes, one of which is in the city.

### Simple Greens – Simply Country
- Over 400 color photographs of country homes decorated for the holidays. Also a chapter on "how to make a country bed" and the recipe for the large decorative gingerbread boys and pantry cakes.

### The Country Life
- The homes of four antique dealers are featured in this book; Marjorie Staufer of Ohio, Colette Donovan, Molly Garland and Kathy Hopper all of Massachusetts. Also included are 2 other homes in Massachusetts, 1 Maine house, 1 New Hampshire home and that of children's book author Mark Kimball Moulton.

### Simply Country Gardens
- Over 500 color photographs of "just country gardens" from twenty-three homes.

### The Spirit of Country
- A house tour format book featuring homes in Virginia, Maine, Connecticut, Indiana, Ohio, Massachusetts, New Hampshire and Kentucky.

### The Joy of Country
- Over 400 pictures including a Wisconsin home, an upstate New York home, a primitive home in Ohio, a Connecticut 18thC home, a doublewide in Delaware, 5 homes in Massachusetts including one on Cape Cod, and one a first period home; a western Pennsylvania home and a Maryland home converted from a 19thC grainery.